How to Recognize Witchcraft

My Personal Testimony from Victim to Victor

Kendra L. Slaughter

NOTE TO ALL READERS

All scriptures are from the New Living Translation (NLT), unless otherwise stated.

satan is in lowercase, unless directly quoted, to avoid giving honor or dignity to the enemy.

The g is lowercase in "god said" to acknowledge that this is not the God that the author believes in or serve.

Credits:
Book cover designed by Gregory C. Austin, Jr.
Photographer: Angela Gudger, CEO of UNeek D Picshun
Hair: Kecia Slaughter and Kema Webster
Makeup: Jessica Slaughter, CEO of "I AM"

Editing by Elizabeth P., CreateSpace Editor

Copyright © 2016 by Kendra L. Slaughter
           All rights reserved.

      ISBN: 1519543085
      ISBN 13: 9781519543080

Website: www.kendra-slaughter.com
Email: kendraslaughter29@gmail.com

In Loving Memory
Of
Pastor Artemus Raye Slaughter

February 12, 1963 – September 22, 2010

This book is in memory of one of my older brothers, the late pastor Artemus Raye Slaughter, who went to be with the Lord on September 22, 2010; the birthdate of my oldest sister, Kim. My brother, affectionately known as Temus, was an anointed pastor, singer, songwriter, and musician who loved people. I miss him so much, but I thank the Lord for the time we had together to share a natural and spiritual journey.

My brother was the founder and pastor of True Praise Church Baptist (TPCB). I was a member of his church in 2007, when I was called into the ministry. While pastoring TPCB, he was elected to be the pastor of my home church, Greater Tabernacle M.B. Church (GTMBC), and TPCB and GTMBC became one family.

My current pastor, John F. Hannah, released me to preach at GTMBC in July 2010 and my brother died two months later. I am so grateful to the Lord for allowing him to hear me preach my first sermon "Women of God United for a Purpose" before he died.

Our family will not forget the legacy he left behind. For the rest of our lives, we will honor him through ministry, song, and caring for people in the same manner he did.

Acknowledgments

First, I have to acknowledge my Lord and savior Jesus Christ, because without Him I am nothing. I thank the Lord for being my savior, my deliverer, my provider, and my source. The Lord is my everything, and I give Him all the glory, honor, and praise! This book is possible because of Him. I can truly say that "didn't nobody do this but God."

I say thank You to my Lord and savior Jesus Christ for giving me this opportunity to share what He has given me. I say thank You to my heavenly Father for choosing me to go through witchcraft. I say thank You, Lord, for this season in my life when I had no other choice but to turn to You and Your unfailing word.

For it was during this season that I read the Bible every day and studied for hours and allowed You and Your precious Holy Spirit to pour into me so that I can pour into others at the appointed time. Thank You, Lord, for placing me in a family that walked with You generations before I was born. Thank You, Lord, for all You've done for me!

Second, I would like to acknowledge some very important and influential people in my life. To my parents and mentors in the ministry, Deacon Emeritus Jimmy L. Slaughter Sr. and Pastor Aridell M. Slaughter: thank you for taking me and my siblings to church and introducing us to Jesus Christ at a young age. You laid the groundwork and foundation for our salvation.

Thank you for introducing us to God, His son, Jesus Christ; and the Holy Spirit. Thank you for teaching us about Christ in your daily walk. Throughout your lives, you have shown us what unconditional love looks like in your covenant marriage of fifty-seven years and by serving in ministry for over forty-five years.

I am truly blessed to have had both of you as the perfect man and woman to show me the way to righteousness and holiness. Thank you for praying for me until the Lord delivered me. Thank you for your spiritual walk and for leading by example. Not only did you sacrifice for our family, you also made sacrifices for others and for the building of God's kingdom.

To my living siblings: Kim, Minister Jimmy Jr., Kecia, Jeffery, Kathy, and Minister Krista: thank you for believing in the God in me and believing in the call that is on my life. It makes a difference when family can celebrate the God in me and the path He has chosen for me.

You were firsthand witnesses while I endured this test. You prayed for me, you forgave me, and the Lord restored our familial relationship in 2007. All the glory belongs to God! I love you, and I thank the Lord for a family that believes in God and the power of prayer. As the youngest sibling, you all have truly spoiled me and shown your love for me in different ways. I am truly blessed by your love and respect!

To my sister Kecia: we have been close since I was a child. When I was young, I shared a bed with you, and you took care of me as if I were your own. We grew to become friends, and the enemy came after our bond and our friendship during this time. I thank the Lord for your willing heart to forgive me, and thanks be to God for restoring our sisterhood and our friendship! Thank you for your love and care for me all of my life.

To my sisters-in-law: Crystal and Tonnette: I thank the Lord for you being one with my brothers and loving them unconditionally! To my nieces and nephews: Paris, Jimmy III, Kesha, Creshawn, Miracle, Lil Terry, and Trayon, Minister Chauntae and Jordin, Jeanine and Trinity, Ashley, Gregory Jr, and Anthony (AJ), Terrance, Nikki and Cameron, DeVonte and Porschia, Jeliyah, Terry Jr. (TJ), Jenesis, Taylor, Tremell and Tinlee, Torry, and Minister KeAndra (my namesake), Elvin IV and Levi, Keturah and Josiah: thank you for the respect you have shown me over the years and for allowing me to pour into your lives. I pray that I have been an example that you can be used by God at any age if you only submit to His will for your life.

To the Slaughter family and the Sims family: thank you for your love and support. I look forward to our family reunions when we come together to have fun and to give praise to our God in song.

To my best friend, David W. Holmes: thank you for being with me the entire time I was going through this test and never letting me go. Despite the numerous times that I told you I could not talk to you while I was being controlled, you were persistent, and you stayed close to me. You covered me and kept up with me no matter what. You are irreplaceable and I love you unconditionally.

  To my pastor, John F. Hannah: when I came into your office in 2008, you believed my testimony, and you believed in the call that was on my life. When I came to New Life Covenant Church Southeast (NLCSE), I was broken, hurt, and confused. I received my healing and deliverance at the altar, through the revelation of His Word in your sermons, and through worship. Thank you for the opportunity to be a minister of the Lord and a servant to the flock that He entrusted to you.

To my servant leaders at NLCSE, Pastor Hill, Ms. Loretta, Pastor Ben, and Minister Hurley: thank you for your guidance in leadership and your example of commitment and faithfulness to the Lord in ministry.

To the ministers of NLCSE: I count it a privilege to serve along with you every week to edify the body of Christ. We get to serve! To the servants of the Greeters Ministry, and the Food Pantry Ministry of NLCSE: it was truly a blessing to lead you as we served together. You are faithful servants who serve the Lord with willing and obedient hearts!

To my divine connections, Willie Mae (Woodie), Miriam, Angela, LaTanya, Kamela,

Shevelle, RoSharon, Davetta (China), and Jermaine (Little Brother): thank you for rejoicing with me, praying with me, and encouraging me on a daily basis. You are my prayer and praise partners and I thank you for your heartfelt and sincere love for me. Kamela and RoSharon: thank you for being my caretakers while I was in the birthing room, and helping me to push toward the promises that the Lord made to me, in spite of the enemy's continuous attacks.

    To those who have shown themselves friendly, Sanora and Shawn (Nephew), Eddie M., Golliday (Pops), Nieta, Joseph, Andre, Thomas, Helen, Benny, Minister Lee, Caulette, and Caprece, Antwaine, Belinda, Glenda, Godparents Dwight and Melinda, Ministers Bill and Kim, Annette and Cynthia, Sharon, Rasheed, and Mona, Val, Debbie, Keith, La Cretia, Shona, DeShon and Ms. Dawson, Tony and Pat, Tyrone and Joan, Jessica and LaTrina, Eddie D., Risha: thank you for your unconditional love and acceptance, your encouragement, your many acts of kindness, and your prayers!

 To my village, the NLCSE church family: it is a joy to worship and praise the Lord with a family who is sold out for Jesus Christ! To my second spiritual mentor, Pastor Sandra Howell: thank you for trusting in the God in me. Thank you for the opportunities that you have given me to use my gifts. To Minister C. Terrell Wheat: thank you for your encouraging words and your prayers in this walk as a minister. I'm excited about your future in your prayer ministry. To Minister Charlom Wilcher: thank you for being there when I needed an ear to hear my pain as the Lord was delivering me and healing me. Thank you for your prayers when I was being delivered!

    I would also like to acknowledge the churches I have belonged to before I joined NLCSE. I was raised in these churches, and they are where I first witnessed my parents and my pastors serving faithfully in ministry: my home church, GTMBC, where my uncle, the late pastor J. B. Sims Jr., was the founder and pastor; New Israelite M. B. Church, under the leadership of the late Rev. Dr. Willie C. Austin; and at TPCB. Thank you to the current pastors and members of these churches, Pastor

Rockett (Greater Tabernacle), and Pastor Alston (New Israelite), for the love and support you have shown me down through the years. I am grateful to the Lord for my Baptist roots and for those who gave me my start in ministry. I thank the Lord for my humble beginnings!

    To the staff at Trinity International University, Dean Dr. Reynolds, Dr. Milner, Dr. Roussell, Dr. April, Dr. Fields, Dr. Van-Gemeren, and Pastor Avril: thank you for teaching the word of God with power, passion, and conviction. I'm grateful that you are a part of my spiritual growth in learning how to study the word of God to show myself approved unto Him.

To Pastor Quentin Mumphery: words cannot express how grateful I am for the knowledge and understanding of the Bible that you poured into me when you taught the ministerial class of 2014 at NLCSE. God bless you and your ministry at New Hope Covenant Church!

To my friend and colleague in the ministry, Rev. Alan B. Conley: I thank the Lord for the wisdom the Lord has blessed you with. I thank you for allowing me to use the revelation that the Lord has given you. I look forward to reading your work in the future. Thank you to all of my extended family and friends for the love of Jesus Christ that you have shown me and my family members.

Contents

Introduction...	1
Chapter 1—What Is Witchcraft?.............................	6
Chapter 2—Witchcraft in the Bible........................	11
Sorcerers..	14
Divination...	16
Test the Spirit...	21
Discernment..	22
Casting Out Evil Spirits.......................................	26
Fortune-Tellers and False Prophets..................	29
Chapter 3—How Did Witchcraft Begin?................	32
Stronghold..	38
Betrayal...	40
Chapter 4—The Fruits of Witchcraft.....................	42
Secrecy..	44
Selfishness..	45
Envy and Jealousy..	46
False Humility..	49
Plots and Planning..	49
Control...	50
Fasting for Control...	51
Isolation..	52
Manipulation..	57
Rituals..	60
Physical Signs..	62
Spiritual Warfare...	63
Traits of Witchcraft..	64
Chapter 5—Who Practices Witchcraft?..................	67
Chapter 6—Deliverance..	72
My Cross..	78
Chapter 7—Restoration..	81
Chapter 8—A New Beginning: Victory in Christ Jesus!	85
Prayers of Forgiveness & Salvation..................	88
Conclusion...	90

Introduction

And they overcame him by the blood of the Lamb and by the word of their testimony, and they did not love their lives to the death.

—Revelation 12:11 (NKJV)

This book is my personal testimony of endurance for a season in my life and how I overcame satan and his plan to destroy me. I am a Christian and I believe in the Bible. I grew up in a Baptist church and was baptized at the age of twelve. I believe that the word of God is the truth, and I try to live my life by that word.

I want to share my testimony with the body of Christ because I believe that a

Christian's testimony should not be hidden but shared with others to encourage them and let them know that they can make it. The enemy tries to keep us in guilt and shame, but the Bible says that there is no condemnation to those who are in Christ Jesus (Rom. 8:1).

There may be someone who needs to hear your testimony because she is facing the same trial you did, and she needs to know that she can go through it and come out victorious with the help of the Lord! Christians should be open to sharing their experiences with others in order to bring knowledge and deliverance through Jesus Christ. Our silence is a tactic that the enemy uses to try to defeat the believers of Jesus Christ.

When Jesus met the woman at the well in John chapter 4, He told her all the things she ever did, and she went to Samaria to tell others. The Samaritans believed in Jesus because the woman at the well shared her testimony. My prayer is that my testimony will cause people to believe in Jesus Christ and to know that the blood He shed on the cross can and will deliver you from anything!

What I offer in this book is the truth. I do not confess to know everything about witchcraft. This is my personal experience and revelation from the Lord Jesus Christ. The Holy Spirit revealed to me that I was under witchcraft. I can testify with Paul in the Bible when he said,

"I received my message from no human source, and no one taught me. Instead, I received it by direct revelation from Jesus Christ" (Gal. 1:12).

This book will give you my insight into what I experienced in a friendship where I was mentally, emotionally, and spiritually abused. I was unstable and did not have confidence in myself or others, and I did not know who I was in Christ. The only person I trusted was the person controlling me. I didn't see her abusive ways, even though others tried to tell me that she was controlling me.

I did not see things clearly until the Lord opened my eyes. It was as if I was asleep for a year and a half, and then one day I finally woke up. The Lord literally took the scales from my eyes. I could finally see what had been there all the time. The Lord broke the chains of bondage, divination, and witchcraft from my life and gave me an overcoming anointing. To God be the glory!

But it was only after I decided to believe what the Lord showed that I became free. After the truth was revealed, I still had a decision to make. Do I continue to believe the lie and go on with life as it was? Or do I accept the truth and deal with the embarrassment and shame? I choose the latter because I realized that a lie keeps you in bondage and the truth sets you free. I chose to embrace the truth and become transparent with God, with myself, and then with others.

Chapter 1

What Is Witchcraft?

You cannot confront what you cannot recognize.

—Dr. Bruce Fields

In order to address any situation, you have to be able to recognize what it is. I was ignorant to what witchcraft was, so when I was confronted with the spirit of witchcraft operating in a friend of mine whom I will name Jan, I submitted to that spirit, not knowing that witchcraft is a tactic of satan.

"So that Satan will not outsmart us. For we are familiar with his evil schemes" (2 Cor. 2:11).

To get an understanding of witchcraft, I will use several definitions.

Merriam-Webster defines *witchcraft* as "magical things that are done by witches: the use of magical powers obtained especially from evil spirits; the use of sorcery or magic; communication with the devil or with a familiar (spirit); an irresistible influence or fascination."

To get a better understanding, I looked up the individual words *witch* and *craft*:

A witch is "a very unpleasant woman."

A craft is "a skill in deceiving to gain an end."

If you combine these definitions, you see that witchcraft is carried out by "a very unpleasant woman who is skilled at deceiving to gain an end."

In *Merriam-Webster*, deceive means "to make (someone) believe something that is not true."

My personal definition of witchcraft is "when a person makes you believe something that is not true, to get what they want—and they will get what they want by any means necessary." The end was always beneficial to Jan, even though it *appeared* that the end was beneficial to me.

Minister Krista Lenon says, "The strength in deception is you don't know that you are being deceived."

I was being deceived and destroyed by witchcraft because of my lack of knowledge about witchcraft (Hos. 4:6).

The *Holman Bible Dictionary* defines a witch as "a female whose work was in divination and magic." The *King James Dictionary* defines a witch as "a woman who, by compact with the devil, practices sorcery or enchantment."

Even though a witch is defined as being a woman, I have also met men who are operating in the spirit of witchcraft. *Merriam-Webster* uses the term *warlock* for men like these.

Witchcraft is grounded in lies and is against the truth. We know that witchcraft comes from satan because scripture says,

"For you are the children of your father the devil, and you love to do the evil things he does. He was a murderer

from the beginning. He has always hated the truth, because there is no truth in him. When he lies, it is consistent with his character; for he is a liar and the father of lies." (John 8:44).

After you read this book, I hope it is clear that witchcraft goes against the word of God and that witchcraft is an abomination to Him.

Chapter 2

Witchcraft in the Bible

Rebellion is as sinful as witchcraft, and stubbornness as bad as worshiping idols. So because you have rejected the command of the Lord, he has rejected you as king.

—*1 Samuel 15:23*

In the passage of scripture above, the Lord rejected Saul as the king of the Israelites because Saul was not obedient to *everything* that God commanded him to do. God told Saul to destroy everything that belonged to the Amalekites (1 Sam. 15:3). But Saul did not destroy everything like God told him to; he only destroyed what was despised and unworthy in *his* eyes while keeping the spoils *he* considered good (1 Sam. 15:9). In other words, Saul did what he wanted to do, and this is rebellion to the Lord! How many times have we been partially obedient to the Lord when He commanded us to do something? Partial or halfway obedience is disobedience, and disobedience to God is as sinful as witchcraft. For scripture says,

"For the person who keeps all of the laws except one is as guilty as a person who has broken all of God's laws" (James 2:10).

We have to trust God and do what He tells us to do because He sees what we cannot see and He knows our future. The Lord's thoughts and His ways are higher than ours (Isa. 55:8–9).

Merriam-Webster defines rebellion as "opposition to one in authority or dominance." When a believer confesses Jesus Christ as his savior, he gives control, authority, and rule to God the Father, to His son, Jesus Christ, and to the Holy Spirit, who are one. A believer of Jesus Christ should not be in opposition to his master, Jesus Christ. When a believer rebels or disobeys what the Lord tells him to do, he is operating in the spirit of witchcraft.

Now I will explain how sorcerers, divination, fortune-tellers, and false prophets are associated with witchcraft in the Bible.

Sorcerers

Who are sorcerers? *Merriam-Webster* defines a sorcerer as "a person who practices sorcery: a wizard or warlock."

What is sorcery? *Merriam-Webster* defines sorcery as "the use of magical powers that are obtained through evil spirits."

Therefore, a sorcerer is "a person who practices sorcery using magical powers obtained through evil spirits."

In Acts 13:1–5, the Holy Spirit appointed Barnabas and Saul, and their assistant John, to preach in Cyprus. Eventually they encountered a sorcerer.

"Afterward they traveled from town to town across the entire island until finally they reached Paphos, where they

met a Jewish sorcerer, a false prophet named Bar-Jesus. He had attached himself to the governor, Sergius Paulus, who was an intelligent man. The governor invited Barnabas and Saul to visit him, for he wanted to hear the word of God. But Elymas, the sorcerer (as his name means in Greek), interfered and urged the governor to pay no attention to what Barnabas and Saul said. He was trying to keep the governor from believing.

"Saul, also known as Paul, was filled with the Holy Spirit, and he looked the sorcerer in the eye. Then he said, 'You son of the devil, full of every sort of deceit and fraud, and enemy of all that is good! Will

you never stop perverting the true ways of the Lord?'" (Acts 13:6–10)

There are three important points to take away from this passage.

- A sorcerer is a false prophet who is full of deceit. He is a fraud, a son of the devil, and the enemy of all righteousness.
- A sorcerer tries to hinder the salvation of others by perverting the straight ways of the Lord.
- The Lord will punish those who hinder His work.

Divination

In Acts 16:1–15, Paul, Silas, and Timothy were on their way to Macedonia to preach the gospel.

"Now it happened, as we went to prayer, that a certain slave girl possessed with a spirit of divination met us, who brought her masters much profit by fortune-telling" (Acts 16:16, NKJV).

Let us break this verse down with definitions from *Merriam-Webster*.

- A slave is "someone who is legally owned by another person and is forced to work for that person without pay; a person is who strongly influenced and controlled by something."
- To be possessed is to be "influenced or controlled by something (as an evil spirit, a passion, or an idea)."
- Divination is "the practice of attempting to foretell future events or discover

hidden knowledge by occult or supernatural means."

- A fortune-teller is "a person who claims to use special powers to tell what will happen to someone in the future: a person who tells people's fortunes."

I will paraphrase this Bible passage according to the definitions for a better understanding:

"This certain slave girl was strongly influenced or controlled by something (as an evil spirit, a passion, or an idea) as she attempted to foretell future events or discover hidden knowledge by occult or supernatural means, using special powers to tell what would happen to someone in the future."

Fortune-telling is not of God. I will talk about fortune-tellers later in this chapter.

"This girl followed Paul and us, and cried out, saying, 'These men are the servants of the Most High God, who proclaim to us the way of salvation.' And this she did for many days. But Paul, greatly annoyed, turned and said to the spirit, 'I command you in the name of Jesus Christ to come out of her.' And he came out that very hour" (Acts 16:17–18, NKJV).

The girl was speaking the truth...but not by the power of the Holy Spirit. She cried out the truth for many days as she followed Paul, Silas, and Timothy. Paul became annoyed.

But why is Paul annoyed if she was stating the truth? It wasn't the truth that annoyed Paul; it was her spirit. Just because someone is telling you the truth does not automatically mean that he or she is operating in the spirit of the living God, which is the Holy Spirit.

How do you know what spirit a person is operating in?

"Dear friends, do not believe everyone who claims to speak by the Spirit. You must test them to see if the spirit they have comes from God. For there are many false prophets in the world" (1 John 4:1).

This scripture shows us that you cannot recognize if a person is a true prophet or a false prophet by their words alone; you must test their spirit. Paul tested the spirit in this girl for many days.

Test the Spirit

How do you test a person's spirit?

Merriam-Webster defines a test as "a critical examination, observation, or evaluation."

Paul did not decide right away that this girl's spirit was evil. He critically examined, observed, or evaluated her spirit for many days. This is a lesson for Christians not to be too quick to say whether or not someone's spirit is of God just because he is telling the truth or because he says "God said!" Ask the Holy Spirit to reveal a person's spirit to you.

"When the Spirit of truth comes, he will guide you into all truth. He will not speak on his own but will tell you what he has heard. He will tell you about the future" (John 16:13).

The Holy Spirit cannot and will not lie to you. The Holy Spirit will lead you to the truth about a person's spirit. Not only that, the Holy Spirit will tell you about your future! You don't need to consult a psychic or a fortune-teller, or read your horoscope. This is what the world does, but Christians should consult the Holy Spirit.

Discernment

Ask the Lord for the gift of discernment. *Merriam-Webster* defines discern as "to detect with senses other than vision; to see or understand the difference."

After the Lord delivered me from the spirit of witchcraft, I asked Him for the gift of discerning of spirits, and he granted me my request. I asked the Lord for this gift because I did not want to be deceived again.

When you have the gift of discernment, you detect with senses other than your eyesight to see or understand the difference between the Holy Spirit and an evil spirit. You have to look with your spiritual eyes!

"But the natural man does not receive the things of the Spirit of God, for they are foolishness to him; nor can he know them, because they are spiritually discerned" (1 Cor. 2:14, NKJV).

After Paul tested her spirit and discerned that she was operating in an evil spirit, he commanded the spirit to come out of the girl in the name of Jesus Christ. Paul recognized the spirit of witchcraft operating in her by her spirit not by her outer appearance or by her words. Paul spoke to the evil spirit in the girl, not to the girl herself.

"For we are not fighting against flesh-and-blood enemies, but against evil rulers and authorities of the unseen world, against mighty powers in this dark world, and against evil spirits in the heavenly places" (Eph. 6:12).

This does not mean that we never confront a person. We have to seek God for wisdom in what to say to someone and when to say it. Matthew 18:15–20 gives us instructtions on how to confront a brother or sister in Christ who has sinned against us. Galatians 6:1–5 shows us how to bear and share the burdens of a sister or brother in Christ. Even after we confront a brother or sister in Christ, we should forgive just as the Lord forgives us (Col. 3:13).

What happens after Paul addressed the spirit in this girl?

"Her masters' hopes of wealth were now shattered, so they grabbed Paul and Silas and dragged them before the authorities at the marketplace. 'The whole city is in an uproar because of these Jews!' they shouted to the city officials. 'They are teaching customs that are illegal

for us Romans to practice'" (Acts 16:19–21).

When you operate in the Lord's purpose for your life, you will cause trouble in the camp of the enemy.

As long as the girl was operating in an evil spirit by fortune-telling, bringing her masters much profit, Paul, Silas, and Timothy were not a threat to her masters.

But when the Lord delivered the girl through Paul, she was no longer profitable to her masters, and the magistrates said that Timothy, Paul, and Silas were troubling their city.

Casting Out Evil Spirits

We have to be sure that we are operating in the power of God when we try to cast evil spirits out of someone. In Acts 19:11-12, God used Paul to work unusual miracles to heal people of diseases and to cast out evil spirits. A group of Jews tried to cast out demons in the name of the Lord Jesus and this is what took place:

"But one time when they tried it, the evil spirit replied, "I know Jesus, and I know Paul, but who are you?" Then the man with the evil spirit leaped on them, overpowered them, and attacked them with such violence that they fled from the house, naked and battered. (Acts 19:15–16).

As the story continues, God was glorified in this situation:

"The story of what happened spread quickly all through Ephesus, to Jews and Greeks alike. A solemn fear descended on the city, and the name of the Lord Jesus was greatly honored. Many who became believers confessed their sinful practices. A number of them who had been practicing sorcery brought their incantation books and burned them at a public bonfire. The value of the books was several million dollars. So the message about the Lord spread widely and had a powerful effect. (Acts 19:17–20).

Merriam-Webster defines incantation as "a use of spells or verbal charms spoken or sung as a part of a ritual of magic; a written or recited formula of words designed to produce a particular effect."

This shows us how the power of God can bring deliverance when He chooses to use us for His glory. When you try to use God for personal glory, there is no change and no deliverance.

Fortune-Tellers and False Prophets

Merriam-Webster defines a fortune-teller as "a person who claims to use special powers to tell what will happen to someone in the future: a person who tells people's fortune; one that professes to foretell future events."

Merriam-Webster defines a prophet as "one who utters divinely inspired revelations; one who foretells future events; one gifted with more than ordinary spiritual and moral insight."

As you can see, a fortune-teller and a prophet both "foretell future events." Here are the differences.

- A fortune-teller
    - claims to use special powers and
    - asks you for money to tell you your future.
- A true prophet of the living God
    - utters divinely inspired revelations;
    - is gifted with more than ordinary spiritual and moral insight— prophecy is a gift from the Lord (1 Cor. 12:10); and
    - prophesies in the name of the Lord Jesus.

How do you know if a person is a true prophet?

"But any prophet who falsely claims to speak in my name or who speaks in the name of another god must die. But you may wonder, 'How will we know whether or not a prophecy is from the Lord?' If the prophet speaks in the Lord's name but his prediction does not happen or come true, you will know that the Lord did not give that message. That prophet has spoken without my authority and need not be feared" (Deut. 18:20–22).

Chapter 3

How Did Witchcraft Begin?

Study to shew thyself approved unto God, a workman that needeth not to be ashamed, rightly dividing the word of truth

—2 Timothy 2:15, KJV

Witchcraft began in my life because of deception and because I did not know the word of God for myself. Jan used the Bible and a lie for her gain. She used the scriptures out of context to get what she wanted and to justify her behavior. Jan began to tell me things that I only spoke to my heavenly Father about, and when she gave me a word, she always said "god said." I thought, Jan must surely be a true prophet because she told me things that I only told the Lord. After this, I believed everything she told me. I put her on a spiritual pedestal, as if she was higher than me spiritually.

    I looked up to her as if she had made it, and I was trying to get to where she is spiritually. From that day forward, I did not question anything she said. What I did not know at that time was that satan is "the prince of the power of the air" (Eph. 2:2).

    Every time Jan gave me a word from the Lord, she always said "god said." But when you speak for God, you also speak for His Son, Jesus Christ (John 5:23). Jan never mentioned Jesus Christ or Lord; she only said "god said." I assumed that when Jan said "god said," she was speaking of the only true and living wise God, but we can make gods out of people, jobs, material things, or a desire.

A god could be any person, thing, or situation that you think about or talk about the most on a given day. You desire this person or thing more than you desire God. Yes the Lord will give us the desires of our hearts; but God is also a jealous God and He will not allow us to have idols or worship someone or something else (Ex. 34:14). All worship, glory, and honor belong to God alone.

"For even if there are so-called gods, whether in heaven or on earth (as there are many gods and many lords), yet for us there is one God, the Father, of whom are all things, and we for Him; and one Lord

Jesus Christ, through whom are all things, and through whom we live" (1 Cor. 8:5–6, NKJV).

If a person always says "god said" and never acknowledges His Son, Jesus Christ, or the Holy Spirit, be careful! Believers must honor not only the Father and Son but also the Holy Spirit. It is important to know that there are many spirits among us, and we cannot assume that when a person says "the spirit," she is talking about the Holy Spirit. She should be so familiar with the Holy Trinity that she can say with assurance when the Holy Spirit is speaking to her. When believers constantly speak of God and never acknowledge His Son, Jesus, or the Holy Spirit, they are denying the essence of who God is. God is three persons, the blessed Trinity.

Throughout this season of my life, I had a feeling that something was just not right with this friendship, but I couldn't figure it out. My spirit was vexed and troubled. As the saying goes, "I just couldn't put my finger on it" and I was not at peace. I had not yet learned how to depend on the Holy Spirit. My natural eyes didn't see anything wrong with our friendship, and I was not mature in the Lord. I was still living on milk and not solid food (1 Cor. 3:2). I also did not know the voice of the Lord (John 10:27).

I was walking in the flesh and could not discern what was taking place in the spirit. I went to church, but I was not close to God. I did not read the Bible on my own. I only read the Bible on Sundays when my pastor preached, or when I went to Bible study. I had not totally surrendered to Him.

I accepted Jesus Christ as my savior, but I still participated in worldly things and was not allowing myself to be led by the Holy Spirit. I was giving in to my flesh every chance I got while still attending church every Sunday. I was not walking in the Spirit; I was fulfilling the lusts of my flesh (Gal. 5:16–26).

Jan told me that "god said" I was her armor bearer, and it was my responsibility to take care of her and her family, while my needs were secondary. I did not test the spirit her words were given in, nor did I pray about it.

We as believers should not just pray about big or important decisions in our lives. We should take every decision and concern to the Lord, no matter how small it is to us (Prov. 3:5–6). But I didn't. This was a lie and I believed it and I began to act on it.

Stronghold

This lie began to have a stronghold in my life.

What is a stronghold? From *Merriam-Webster,* I will define the words individually then combine them:

Strong is "having a lot of strength"

Hold is "to keep under restraint"

A stronghold is something "that has a lot of strength to keep you under restraint."

Restraint is "a way of limiting, controlling, or stopping something."

This stronghold in my life was a powerful force that controlled me, and kept me away from the truth, from my freedom in Christ Jesus and from other people. I was entangled in bondage. Every decision I made was based on a lie; fulfilling Jan's and her family's needs before my own.

In essence, I made Jan my god for a season because I didn't take anything to the Lord. If Jan said it, I believed it. I submitted to the spirit of witchcraft operating in her. I believed this lie, and I gave the spirit in her the authority to control and manipulate me; which I will discuss later.

Jan was a friend I'd met in church who was appointed by God to betray me. Jesus knew that Judas was on assignment to betray Him so that the will of the Lord would be fulfilled in His life (Matt. 26:47-56).

Betrayal

Yes, your betrayer can be your friend. When David was betrayed, he said,

"If an enemy were insulting me, I could endure it; if a foe were rising against me, I could hide. But it is you, a man like myself, my companion, my close friend, with whom I once enjoyed sweet fellowship at the house of God, as we walked about among worshipers" (Ps. 55:12–14, NIV).

Because Jan was my close friend, I began to tell her secrets about myself and my family. She began to use these secrets and other fruits of witchcraft to keep me in bondage. I encountered the fruits of secrecy, selfishness, envy, jealousy, false humility, plots, planning, control, fasting for control, isolation, manipulation, and rituals. I will also discuss physical signs and traits of witchcraft.

Chapter 4

The Fruits of Witchcraft

Beware of false prophets who come disguised as harmless sheep but are really vicious wolves. You can identify them by their fruit, that is, by the way they act. A good tree produces good fruit, and a bad tree produces bad fruit. Yes, just as you can identify a tree by its fruit, so you can identify people by their actions.

—Matthew 7:15–16a, 17 & 20

Just because someone attends church every week and knows the Bible does not mean he is saved and operating in the spirit of the living God. The Bible shows us that satan knows the word of God (Matt. 4:6). I was expecting false prophets to be in the world, not in the church.

How do you know if a person is really a Christian? By their fruits.

"But the Holy Spirit produces this kind of fruit in our lives: love, joy, peace, patience, kindness, goodness, faithfulness, gentleness, and self-control. There is no law against these things!" (Gal. 5:22–23).

Christians who follow Jesus will exhibit these fruits in their daily lives and their conversations. We need the Holy Spirit to guide our lives so that we will not do what our sinful nature wants.

"The sinful nature wants to do evil, which is just the opposite of what the

Spirit wants. When you follow the desires of your sinful nature, the results are very clear: sexual immorality, impurity, lustful pleasures, idolatry, sorcery, hostility, quarreling, jealousy, outbursts of anger, selfish ambition, dissension, division, envy, drunkenness, wild parties, and other sins like these. Let me tell you again, as I have before, that anyone living that sort of life will not inherit the Kingdom of God" (Gal. 5:17a, 19–21).

Secrecy

My conversations with Jan were secret. *Merriam-Webster* defines a secret as "keeping information hidden from others." When Jan and I were operating in secrecy, no one could know our conversations or what I was going through, because then I would be exposing the spirit of witchcraft.

"For all that is secret will eventually be brought into the open, and everything that is concealed will be brought to light and made known to all (Luke 8:17).

Selfishness

People who practice witchcraft are selfish and impatient, and they only look out for themselves. They want what they want, and they want it immediately. Nothing we do should be done for selfish reasons or selfish gain (Phil. 2:3–4).

When Jan was controlling me, she said I needed to be a giver, but I was only giving to her. I was not giving to others; I only sowed seeds in her, and I always wondered why I did not reap a harvest from these seeds. There was no harvest because the root of my giving was controlled by someone else. I did not give freely.

"You must each decide in your heart how much to give. And don't give reluctanly or in response to pressure. For God loves a person who gives cheerfully" (2 Cor. 9:7).

Envy and Jealousy

Jan had a spirit of envy and jealousy, and she wanted what I had. When people have a spirit of envy and jealousy, they want to be you. They will do things like wear their hair like yours, because they are trying to imitate you, just like satan tries to imitate God. They are deceitful and try to destroy you because they cannot be you.

They do not realize that the more they focus on you, the less they see their own uniqueness and they fail to seek God's call and His purpose in their lives.

Jan did not grow up in a two-parent home, nor did she have siblings who grew up in the same house. The Lord blessed me with both of those things. She was sexually abused by a family member, so she sought to control everyone around her. She did not seek help or get deliverance from her issues. As a matter of fact, Jan tried to have a sexual relationship with me, but the Lord said no! Jan was still hurting from the abuse she'd gone through; she was only doing what she knew. She was operating in the generational curse of her family.

In Jan's eyes, my family looked like the Brady Bunch, even with all of our problems. She wanted to destroy my family unit because she didn't have it. But what the enemy did during this season set me up for ministry today, just as the Lord did for Joseph when Joseph's brothers sold him into slavery.

"You intended to harm me, but God intended it all for good. He brought me to this position so I could save the lives of many people" (Gen. 50:20).

False Humility

Jan always acted like she was humble, but in reality she was puffed up with pride (Col. 2:18). She believed everything she did was right; she was never wrong, and she was my teacher. There was nothing I could teach her. She treated me like I was her child; she would check my clothes and hair before I would leave her house to make sure I was presentable.

Plots and Planning

I learned from my experience with witchcraft that the enemy will give people plots. Jan always had a plan for how she was going to get what she wanted. There was no leading of the Holy Spirit. Christians should not be involved in plotting evil against another person.

"Hide me from the secret plots of the wicked, from the rebellion of the workers of iniquity" (Ps. 64:2, NKJV).

Control

Merriam-Webster's definition of control is "to direct the behavior of (a person or animal); to cause (a person or animal) to do what you want." Jan wanted to control every aspect of my life. But no one can take control over you. You give them the power to control you. When a person seek to have power over you, he wants to separate you from your family, friends, and everyone you are familiar with;

because he wants you to become familiar with his spirit and do what he tells you to do.

The Bible tells us to have self-control, not control of others. I allowed Jan to control who I talked to and when I talked to them. I also allowed her to control my money. When I got paid, I gave my money to her, and she told me what I was going to do with it.

Fasting for Control

I fasted and lost a lot of weight during this season, but I did not look well because it was a fast from hell. We fasted, we did not fast and pray as the scriptures tell believers to do (Mark 9:29). Jan would call a fast to make sure that I was still under her control. She also called a fast when she wanted something.

These fasts were selfish in nature and similar to the fast that Jezebel called when she murdered Naboth for control of his vineyard in 1 Kings 21:1-16. Jezebel practiced witchcraft (2 Kings 9:22), and her motive for the fast was to go against God.

When someone asks you to fast, she may be asking under false pretenses. When you fast, are you pleasing man, or are you pleasing God? Fasting that pleases God is described in Isaiah chapter 58. Pray to the Lord for guidance when someone asks you to fast.

Isolation

Isolation is a sign that someone is trying to control you. Jan isolated me from my family and friends. When someone tries to get you to turn from your family and close friends, beware! Jan used my weaknesses against me and suggested that my family was the cause of my problems. She hinted that her family should become my family and that I should not talk to my blood family anymore—I should abandon them.

It was Jan's desire to alienate me from anything or anyone that was normal or familiar in my life. She knew that if I talked to my family or friends, they might change my mind and talk some sense into me. Like the man who returned to his family in Luke 15:17-18, I might come to myself or my senses and go back home to my family.

Jan led me to believe that everything I experienced in my childhood was not good enough and that I was deficient in various areas because of my upbringing. When a person is trying to pull you away from your family, he could be operating in a spirit of witchcraft. There is no perfect family. Besides, the Lord put our families together by His design and His perfect will.

I'm not saying that anyone should stay in a familial relationship with someone that is abusive. I'm not saying that you should accept behavior from your family that is not Christlike. But what I am saying is that families go through seasons, and the Lord will show you how to deal with the family that *He* gave you. You should allow the Lord to lead you in everything you do. As believers we say that the Lord does not make mistakes. Well, when it comes to our families, that's still true—He does not make mistakes.

So what did I do? I stopped talking to my family. I didn't attend family reunions or gatherings. I stopped talking to my sister Kecia, and that hurt her because we were so close. I was only allowed to talk to family members on the phone if Jan was right next to me to make sure I didn't say anything wrong. If I did, she told me about it when I hung up. My brother Jimmy even came to one of the deliverance services with me that I attended every week. He wanted to see what was going on with me because I was not acting like myself.

My family members are not always on speaking terms with each other, but they are still my family regardless of any situation and circumstance.

Dr. Aridell Slaughter says, "It's okay to fall out, as long as you fall back in."

Yes, we have moments when we are upset with each other and don't communicate, but we should be open to reconciliation.

"Therefore, if you bring your gift to the altar, and there remember that your brother has something against you, leave your gift there before the altar, and go your way. First be reconciled to your brother, and then come and offer your gift" (Matt. 5:23–24, NKJV).

I could talk to my family members when Jan was around, but under no circumstances could I talk to my best friend, David, because she said he was out to get me. Therefore I would hide and call David using *67 so he would not have my number.

On occasions I would forget to use *67, and he would begin to call me. Jan would be upset, so I had to change my cell phone number. I changed my number three times because I continued to talk to David. When he couldn't reach me, he would just drive by my house or Jan's house. He always found a way to keep up with me.

Manipulation

Merriam-Webster defines manipulation as "to control or play upon by artful, unfair, or insidious means especially to one's own advantage." Manipulation occurs when a person makes hints or suggestions about what he wants you to do. This is a form of mind control. When a person attempts to manipulate you, he "beats around the bush" instead of being forward and direct, or he makes a suggestion or a hint as to what he wants.

For example, suppose you are sitting at the table with someone. You would like a drink of water, but you do not want to get up and get it. So you say, "I am thirsty. I would really like a bottle of water." Or you may say, "I don't feel like getting up, but I would really like a bottle of cold water." You are trying to manipulate the other person to get the water for you. You are waiting on them to offer to get what you want. All you had to do was ask the person to get you a bottle of water—or better yet, get up and get the water yourself!

Jan used this kind of manipulation a lot. She would often make hints and suggestions to me during conversations, or she would say, "If I were you, I would do this." Then I would offer to do what she "suggested."

Jan also used manipulation when she wanted something from me that I did not want to do. It was hard for me to say no to Jan in the first place. Jan knew how I wanted to be obedient to the Lord, so when she wanted something really badly, she would say "god said."

Rev. Alan B. Conley says, "Stop forging God's signature on your lies...that's called manipulation."

Rituals

I do not know all of the rituals that are performed when a person is practicing witchcraft, but I can tell you the experience I had. There was an instance where Jan told me to close my eyes. After a few minutes, with my eyes still closed, I went into the spirit realm and saw a person's home in a suburb. I was in Jan's living room, but I could literally see into someone else's home.

I described the home to Jan's daughter, who had been to that house. I cannot explain to you how it happened. All I know is that I could accurately describe a home I had never physically been in. This was the only time in my life that I ever experienced this. I have not tried to do this again because it occurred when I was under the influence of witchcraft, and I know that God was not pleased.

Candles were very significant in witchcraft. Most of the time at night, the entire house would be lit with candles only, with no other lights on. There was an instance in when Jan put her hand on top of the flame of a lit candle, and she was able to keep her hand there for a couple of minutes without feeling the heat. I tried to do the same thing and I was not able to keep my hand on the flame for five seconds. I'm not sure what this meant; or what significance this played in witchcraft, but I was not able to master this.

Physical Signs

There were some physical challenges that I endured. I was the only one in the house that was constantly sick and had medical problems that were unexplainable. I had headaches all the time. It was a piercing pain that I can't accurately describe. The headaches were not curable with medicine, nor could they be explained by doctors. They were spiritual.

The headaches were a constant reminder that I was being controlled in my mind. I did not have a sound mind and my actions and behaviors followed my controlled state of mind. Even today, I have the same headaches to let me know that witchcraft is present or I am being attacked in the spirit realm. Back then, I didn't know what to do.

Spiritual Warfare

Today, when these headaches come upon me, I am in spiritual warfare and I have to fight. How do I fight? I worship, I pray, I pray in the spirit, I sing, I sing in the spirit, I anoint my head, I quote the Word of God, I play worship music and I plead the blood of Jesus over my life.

"For the weapons of our warfare are not carnal, but mighty through God to the pulling down of strong holds" (2 Cor. 10:4, KJV)

I lost a drastic amount of weight and I looked unhealthy. I looked sick and depleted.

Regardless to how much sleep I got, I would still wake up tired and drained. I realized that I was in a deep state of depression with no will to live, no strength, no energy and no desire to do better. Witchcraft literally sucks the life out of you.

Traits of Witchcraft

Below are traits that I experienced in Jan and myself during this time:

- My best was never good enough for Jan
- I lived to please Jan, and for her approval
- I felt like I was always walking on eggshells, I did not want to make

Jan upset with me; it was all about her happiness at my expense
- I was afraid to break away from her; fear is not of God
- I did not have free will; Jan knew where I was at all times
- I was a "yes man" to her. It was difficult for me to tell Jan "no"! I did majority of what she asked me to do. When I did not want to meet her demands, I created an excuse instead of simply saying no
- I didn't have a right to challenge her, because she was the spiritual teacher and I was the student
- She talked to me as if I did not know anything, and I needed her

guidance and direction in every aspect of my life

- I did not have my own personal space; there was no me time
- If I did not answer her phone call right away, she would keep calling me until I answered. Then I would have to explain to her why I didn't answer the phone when she called me the first time
- Jan always criticized me; I could always do better

Chapter 5

Who Practices Witchcraft?

When you enter the land the LORD your God is giving you, be very careful not to imitate the detestable customs of the nations living there. For example, never sacrifice your son or daughter as a burnt offering. And do not let your people practice fortune-telling, or use sorcery, or interpret omens, or engage in witchcraft, or cast spells, or function as mediums or psychics, or call forth the spirits of the dead. Anyone who does these things is detestable to the LORD. It is because the other nations have done these detestable things that the LORD your God will drive them out ahead of you. But you must be blameless before the LORD your God. The nations you are about to displace consult sorcerers and fortune-tellers, but the LORD your God forbids you to do such things.

—Deuteronomy 18:9–14

As we can see from this scripture, the Lord told the Israelites to avoid these wicked customs. The Lord makes it clear that witchcraft is not of Him. Any person can operate in the spirit of witchcraft if she chooses to.

Witchcraft is what the world operates in and should not be named among us in the church. The children of God should practice righteousness and holiness not witchcraft (1 John 2:29). If a believer is operating in a spirit of witchcraft, pray for that person. Pray that the Lord will create in him a clean heart and renew the right spirit within him (Ps. 51:10), and pray for his deliverance (2 Sam. 22:2).

Sometimes witchcraft is spread from generation to generation. As children, we may have been taught behaviors and practices that are not in agreement with the Bible. When we are ignorant, the Lord has mercy on us, but when we are taught that something is not right to do and we do it anyway, then the Lord judges us, and ignorance is no longer an excuse.

"Remember, it is sin to know what you ought to do and then not do it." (James 4:17)

We as believers cannot be so spiritual that we think we cannot be deceived. Even the elect can be deceived (Matt. 24:24). People can deceive you, and you can also deceive yourself.

"But be ye doers of the word, and not hearers only, deceiving your own selves (James 1:22, KJV).

The enemy is tactical and purposeful. He attacks with a purpose because he is a copycat. He desires to be God, and He desires to do what God does. This is the reason satan fell from heaven and was cast into hell (Isa. 14:12–15).

Why do people practice witchcraft? For selfish reasons; some want power, some want to be in control, some want to be a god, some want fame, and some want money and to be rich. The eternity of Christians who practice witchcraft is very clear in the Bible.

"But cowards, unbelievers, the corrupt, murderers, the immoral, those who practice witchcraft, idol worshipers, and all liars—their fate is in the fiery lake of burning sulfur. This is the second death" (Rev. 21:8).

Chapter 6

Deliverance

And the Lord will deliver me from every evil work and preserve me for His heavenly kingdom. To Him be glory forever and ever. Amen!
—2 Timothy 4:18 (NKJV)

I was sent in the enemy's camp to learn his ways so that I can recognize his tactics and pray against them. Every week, I visited a church in Chicago that was operating in a spirit of witchcraft. Even though I didn't join this church, I learned about deliverance, the sound of a witch, and the actions of a person who is being delivered from the spirit of witchcraft.

The time had come for me to be delivered. I was rarely at my own home. I practically lived with Jan. We shared clothes, and most of my furniture was at her house. My deliverance began when a friend of Jan's came to her house and asked me where Jan had gotten all of this furniture. I told the friend that the furniture was mine. She said to me, "This is not God."

I was perplexed and confused. I went home and I cried out to the Lord and I told Him that I needed Him, I needed answers. After I prayed, I literally "woke up." I felt like I had been in a daze. I looked around me and wondered what I had been doing for the past year and a half. The Lord told me that everything I had done in that time was not of Him! I said to the Lord, "If it was not You, then who was it?" That's when the Holy Spirit revealed to me that I was under a demonic spirit of witchcraft. I was devastated, embarrassed, and ashamed, because I thought I was following the leading of the Lord.

The Holy Spirit began to reveal to me what witchcraft was. I reevaluated my entire life, and I became angry. I became angry at God and Jan. How could God, who loves me so much, allow me to be made a fool of in this way? Why would Jan do this to me? I did not take any blame for my part of being a victim of witchcraft.

One day I got so angry that I called Jan and told her I was coming to get my stuff back. I called David and asked him to help me.

He had to work, but his nephews helped me. I rented a U-Haul truck and got some of my clothes and my furniture back from Jan.

Then I began to read the word of God and other books on witchcraft. I was in the Bible for hours every day. This situation brought me to read the Word like I should, and I learned the voice of the Lord through this process.

Meanwhile, Jan called me every day. I did not answer her calls. Then one day I answered the phone and I felt myself being pulled back under her control. After that phone call, I realized that I could not talk to her anymore. I had to literally cut off all communication with her, run for my life and not look back. I was finally free. The Lord opened the door for me to leave. Why would I return to what had me bound?

After I began to read the Bible, I realized that my anger should not have been directed at God or Jan. I was really angry at myself. Why? Because I was not in the Word of God like I should have been. I would have known that satan uses people for his advantage.

"For such *are* false apostles, deceitful workers, transforming themselves into apostles of Christ. And no wonder! For Satan himself transforms himself into an angel of light. Therefore it is no great thing if his ministers also transform themselves into ministers of righteousness, whose end will be

according to their works (2 Cor. 11:13–15, NKJV).

I attended NLCSE's annual sunrise service on a Saturday in September 2006. The anointing was so high that I had my face in the sand, crying out to God, telling Him that I need Him, and I didn't care what I looked like. In my mind I believed the anointing was high because we were outside. Surely all Sunday morning services were not like this. So I went to NLCSE the next day. Guess what? The anointing was still there, and I was at the altar every Sunday after that, being delivered.

I joined NLCSE in September 2006, and I continued to be at the altar and chase after God. One of the ministers at the church, Minister Charlom, gave me her phone number.

One day I was depressed and having a hard time dealing with being a victim of witchcraft and I called her. In the background I could hear her daughter Asia crying, but Minister Charlom did not get off the phone with me. She stayed on the phone and prayed with me. She was sensitive enough in the spirit to know that I was at the lowest point in my life and needed her ear and her prayer.

My Cross

Pastor John F. Hannah says, "Your testimony is your cross."

The cross that I was given was witchcraft. At the beginning of my deliverance, I bore the fruits of anger, embarrassment, frustration, blame, guilt, and condemnation. As

I began to read the word of God and fast and pray for the bonds of wickedness to be loosed off of my life, the fruits from my tree changed to joy and peace.

What fruits are you bearing from the cross that you have been given?

If we carry our cross with grace while trusting God, He will give us what we need to endure until the end. My cross was for my good because I loved God and I was called according to His purpose (Rom. 8:28).

"For I reckon that the sufferings of this present time are not worthy to be compared with the glory which shall be revealed in us" (Romans 8:18, KJV).

I didn't see how God was going to get the glory out of this situation when I was going through. But today I can say that the suffering that I endure while being on the cross of witchcraft, was set up and designed just for me. I can speak, teach, and testify about witchcraft and spiritual warfare all to the Glory of God.

Chapter 7

Restoration

"In his kindness God called you to share in his eternal glory by means of Christ Jesus. So after you have suffered a little while, he will restore, support, and strengthen you, and he will place you on a firm foundation."

—1 Peter 5:10

My flesh did not feel good going through this process from deliverance to restoration and I became bitter. But I thank the Lord for His strength that allowed me to endure until the end. I came out of witchcraft a better person than when I went in. However, I went through a process to go from bitter to better.

"Better is the end of a thing than the beginning thereof: and the patient in spirit is better than the proud in spirit" (Ecc. 7:8, KJV).

I was restored back to God by reading His word and meditating on Him every day. My daily worship songs to the Lord were "You Are God Alone," by Marvin Sapp, and Martha Munizzi's "I Know the Plans I Have for You" and "Your Latter will be Greater." I had to let the Lord know that I trusted His plan and that He is the only God and I put Him back on throne in my heart and in my life.

"King eternal, immortal, invisible, the only wise God, be honour and glory for ever and ever. Amen" (1 Timothy 1:17, KJV).

I didn't understand it then, but now I know that the Lord had a plan for allowing me to go through this season in my life. This test caused me to trust in Him and His unfailing Word, to read and study my Bible daily, to forgive people continuously, to help people, and to pray for people without looking for anything in return.

I also listened to CD recordings of Pastor Hannah's sermons, which I received from my friend and co-worker at the University of Illinois, Willie (Woodie) Ghoston. Willie was a member of NLCSE and she gave me these CDs two years before I listened to them. The Lord knew I would need them!

Now that my personal restoration was complete. I had to be restored with my family and friends. This process began in January 2007, when the Lord led me to join TPCB. I worshipped there with my family for the entire year. In February 2008, the Lord led me back to NLCSE along with my sister Kecia and her three children. Since that time, the Lord led my oldest sister Kim, a niece, cousins, my best friend David, and former members of my previous church to join NLCSE as well.

Chapter 8

A New Beginning: Victory in Christ Jesus!

But thanks be to God, which giveth us the victory through our Lord Jesus Christ.

—1 Corinthians 15:57 (KJV)

My new beginning in Christ is to be a light in the midst of darkness as a minister of the Gospel, and a servant of the Lord who is gentle to all, able to teach, patient, and humble (2 Tim. 2:24–26).

I've learned how to pray for Jan as the Bible instructs us, for "God desires for all men to be saved and to come to the knowledge of the truth" (1 Tim. 2:3–4). The Lord also taught me how to forgive Jan, but that does not mean

I have to go out to eat with her or be her friend again. The Bible says,

"Now I urge you, brethren, note those who cause divisions and offenses, contrary to the doctrine which you learned, and avoid them" (Rom. 16:17, NKJV).

There is a saying: "Your misery is your ministry." This means that the very thing you thought you couldn't get out of, or the one thing that made you miserable or humbled you to the point where you cried out to God, is the very thing that the Lord will use in you for His Glory.

Witchcraft was worse than my process of divorce after being married for 10 years. Yet, I thank the Lord for choosing me to go through this experience. I pray that believers all over the world will yield to the Holy Spirit, say yes to the Lord and His will, resist the devil, and *remain* free in Christ Jesus.

If the Holy Spirit has revealed to you that you have been a victim of witchcraft, or if you are practicing witchcraft yourself, you can have a new beginning in Christ Jesus today. Just like the Lord granted mercy on me, He grants mercy on all.

Today can be a day of newness for you. But if you choose to continue to practice witchcraft and fortune-telling, this is what the Lord says:

"I will put an end to all witchcraft, and there will be no more fortune-tellers" (Mic. 5:12).

If you desire to be set free from the bondage of witchcraft, recite this prayer:

Prayer of Forgiveness

Heavenly Father, I am your child. I ask you to forgive me for submitting to the spirit of witchcraft. I submit to You, and I resist the devil, and now the devil has to flee from me. I choose to live in holiness and righteousness. I choose to obey the Holy Spirit. I renounce the spirit of witchcraft, divination, sorcery, and the like in my life, in my family, and in my bloodline. I cancel all generational curses in my bloodline. The spirit of witchcraft and divination stops here, and I cover my family with the blood of Jesus Christ. We will not practice witchcraft, and we will not be victims of witchcraft. Thank you, Heavenly Father, for being faithful and just to forgive me for my sins and to cleanse me from all unrighteousness. Create in me a clean heart, and renew the right spirit within me. Help me to renew my mind so that I will not even remember how to practice witchcraft. I ask you to give me the mind of Christ. I ask you to help me to think on things are lovely, pure, of good report, and praiseworthy. In Jesus's name, Amen!

"Do right and right will follow" – The Late J.B. Sims, Sr.

If you have not accepted the Lord Jesus as your personal savior and you want to receive Him into your life today, to ensure you spend eternity with God in heaven, recite this prayer:

Prayer of Salvation

Heavenly Father, I am a sinner in need of a savior. According to Your Word in Romans 10:9, I confess with my mouth and believe in my heart that Your Son Jesus died for me, and You raised Him from the dead. Because of my confession and my belief, I am Your child, I am saved, and I will spend eternity with you. In Jesus Name, Amen!

Conclusion

I thank God that we can go to Him in prayer and He will come and see about us! Prayer saved my life and prayer is our vehicle to communicate with the Lord, and to have a relationship with Him. I pray that my testimony will encourage you to share your story, for His Glory!

From Victim to Victor..................

"Didn't Nobody do this but God!"

Made in the USA
Coppell, TX
09 September 2020